A Kid From Akron, Ohio's

Vietnam

Story

A Journey From

Innocence

To

Mental Illness

JEFFREY COCHRAN
ZIA EUBANKS

Itoya Vista Dreams Production
hello@gottacre8.com

Printed n the United States of America.
First Printing: March 2021

ISBN: 978-0-9992133-4-6

Jeff's Dedication

For my son, Scott Cochran

For my sisters,
Debbie Bonomo
Sandy Pendleton
Kathy DeMarko

Zia's Dedication

For my husband and friend,
Jeff Cochran

Fullfilling a promise I made to him 20 years ago to help him tell his story.

May he finally rest in peace.

Acknowledgements

Elisha Eubanks
Chris Mitchell
Axel Mitchell
Isabella Mitchell
Marilyn Markovich
Ginny Eckstein
Don and Kate Franks
Jennifer Franks
Mike and Tippy Cochran

A Special Thank You

To Jeff's sister, Sandy Pendleton for moving to Palm Springs to help care for Jeff the last year of his life. Her love for her brother was deeply felt by him, and everyone in his life. Her presence was appreciated more than she will ever know.

Table Of Contents

"The soldier above all others prays for peace, for it is the soldier who must suffer and bear the deepest wounds and scars of war."

- Douglas MacArthur

Why This Book?

I've put this book together for Jeff. He wanted to be understood by those he loved, but he had no idea how to tell the story. He talked about it often and knew that his family saw him as they wanted to remember him as a kid and teenager, but there was more he wanted them to know.

The boy they knew and loved, who went off to fight in the Vietnam War, was not the same boy who returned. And he never would be. They saw it, and he felt it. He couldn't fully understand it, so he didn't expect them to. It took him decades to begin to grasp what Vietnam had done to him. But during those beginning years of struggling with Post Traumatic Stress Disorder (PTSD) he tried to hide it from them. Playing the "tough guy" and shutting down his feelings was his modus operandi. It worked for him, some of the time.

As time moved on, and he began to get help through the Vet Center counseling and support groups, he became more interested in telling his story.

In 2000, as a Winter Solstice gift I gave him a "gift certificate" to help him organize his Vietnam memories and put them into a book for family and others who may be interested. (We stopped celebrating Christmas and began honoring the season at the Winter Solstice partly because of all the triggers for him. He had been wounded and spent Christmas in the hospital while in Vietnam.) He was excited about the idea of writing his biography. On several occasions we made plans and wrote outlines and talked about what he wanted to convey. However, his PTSD always got in the way. Exploring the memories always triggered his symptoms, so we kept putting it on the backburner.

Here is the certificate I gave to him. The front was a mockup of a book cover and inside I wrote out what I was offering as my gift.

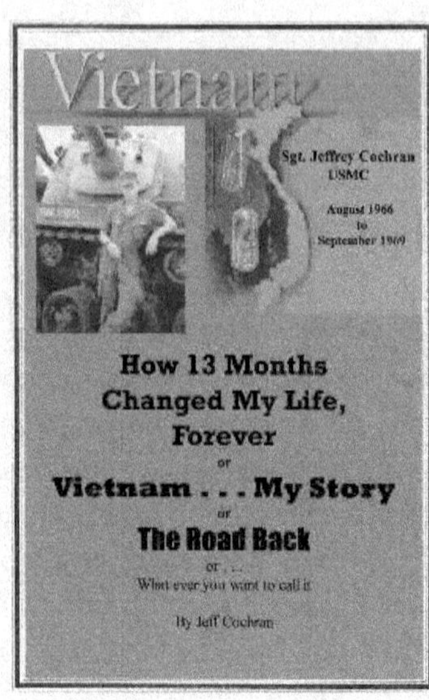

Happy Winter Solstice

TO: Jeff

From: Cindy

My gift to you this Solstice is to help you go through your Vietnam pictures and memorabilia. To save the pictures that you have, identify the people and places. Repair the pictures that are damaged. And make copies of all the pictures to preserve the history of your life.

This gift is a commitment to prepare a written history of your time in Vietnam as a way for you to share you story with your children and your loved ones. By doing this it will allow us and them to heal from this war and capture your history for the future - for your grandchildren and beyond.

We can work on this however your feel comfortable. I am ready, willing and able to be your biographer. Your story needs to be told.

Semper Fi

Love, Cindy

12/2000

Now that he has made his transition, I feel it is more important than ever to tell his story. I am fulfilling my promise. This book is in both my words and his.

Who Was Jeff?

Jeff was a deep thinker and a very spiritually connected man. He resonated with the Buddhist teachings that he saw from the people of Vietnam living in the villages they were fighting to protect from the North Vietnamese. He immediately recognized how wrong the war was and how these people's peaceful, spiritual existence was being destroyed. It was an awakening for him. One that he didn't fully understand at the time, but one he came to embrace as he evolved and grew.

He studied the Buddhist philosophy and had an admiration for the teachings. His experience of the culture while in Vietnam opened his eyes to new ways of thinking and understanding life. He came home with a reverence for life and an expanded view of the world and politics. Some of it good and some of it no so good.

There is a Jeff that not many people knew. Fortunately, I was lucky enough to know that Jeff. The gentle, spiritual, compassionate, and extremely wounded man. He showed me all those aspects of himself. At times, the wounded part became so dominate that it made our relationship very difficult and contributed to two separations over the years. But the other times, when he opened up from behind the wounds and allowed me to see the "real" Jeff, created a deep bond that held us tightly together. It is this side of him that I know he wanted his family to see but didn't have the emotional ability to show it. It was a level of vulnerability that made him very uncomfortable. Plus, it required accepting the PTSD and all that it entailed.

On the other hand, Jeff always told me that he felt that people just hoped he would "get over it." That no one really wanted to know his truth. He had roles – as a son, father, big brother, and uncle – that required, in his mind, pushing all that into the background. He wanted people to be comfortable around him, not afraid of "setting him off." He told me many times that his family "didn't want to hear about it." However, it was one of his greatest desires – to have an open conversation about his experience in Vietnam and how it changed him. The more he understood it, the more he wanted to explain it to those he loved, especially his son and his brother and sisters.

After Jeff made his transition, I found a set of journals he kept in 2001. After reading them, I knew that I had to share them. It is a glimpse of the Jeff I am talking about, the one most people didn't see. I have included it word for word. My hope is that by making this book I can fulfill his desire to be known by his family. It will never be enough, but I hope this helps them to know him on a new level.

The thing that stopped him time and time again was the fear. He was clear that, in his family, talking about intimate feelings was not something encouraged. To the contrary, he often said that staying on a surface level was the safest way to navigate his family. Learning to talk about his feelings or even allow his feelings to have a voice took years of therapy. He didn't expect his family to suddenly open up to hearing his truth.

It's very complicated. PTSD, to the level Jeff suffered from it, is an all-encompassing illness that effects every aspect of life. He would never be able to "recover" from it, but he did learn to manage it from time to time. Like any chronic illness, it required attention, and when he tried to ignore it, it always came at him with a vengeance. Watching him suffer and trying to help him was both heart wrenching and aggravating. There were times when he was open and shared his feelings, and other times he shut down and escaped like a turtle hiding in its shell. So, finding a time or situation to talk to his family about it was very tricky and, ultimately, never happened.

On behalf of Jeff, I am putting this together in hopes that he may be known in the way he wished. I understand that there are members of his family that see me as influencing him (and not in a good way). We used to laugh about that. He knew they felt that way too. We laughed because we knew the arguments and fights we got into over our differing ideals of life and politics, which they never witnessed. Jeff was stubborn as the day is long, and changing his mind about something took some doing, if at all. He was his own man, contrary to what people thought. He was a wise man and would "contemplate" things long and hard before he came to a conclusion. Honestly, it used to drive me crazy! But it was a quality I greatly respected.

Part of the disservice Jeff enacted towards his family was keeping up the "image" of the tough guy Marine. That was the facade he created as a way of coping with his PTSD. One of his greatest regrets was not allowing his son to see the other parts of him. The guy he presented to his son his entire life was not the entirety of Jeff. He felt most comfortable being that persona and felt he had no other choice. He apologized over and over again for not being a good father. It was a safe version of him that felt comfortable for both of them. In his eyes and heart, he knew he wasn't being honest with his son and realized that he had withheld a very deep emotional part of himself from his son. It fell on deaf ears because his son saw him as good father. This created a sadness in Jeff that he could never overcome. It creates a complicated set of dynamics when people can't be their true self with the ones they love the most.

My hope is that, by reading this and hearing Jeff's words, you may know him in a new way. A quote that Jeff and I chose to live by is from Dr. Wayne Dyer, "Keep a mind that is open to everything and attached to nothing." If you read this with an open mind, you may see a part of Jeff you've never seen before.

But please don't feel sad. That isn't what he wanted. He wanted to be understood. For people to see that war had damaged him in ways he couldn't completely overcome. It was war that did it to him. He was not weak or fragile, on the contrary, he had suffered unfathomable horrors and survived physically but was emotionally devastated. That is what Post Traumatic Stress Disorder is all about. It is a mental illness. It creates an illness in the mind that has profound effects on living life. There was no way he could ever return to the innocent 19-year-old kid that left Akron, Ohio for boot camp on August 16, 1966.

Beginning at the End

Starting at the end of someone's life seems like an odd place to begin a book. However, this isn't a biography, this is picture into a life. A story of the untold that needs to be told.

On May 30, 2018, Jeff left this earthly plane. His death certificate says he died of complications from his battle with diabetes, which his exposure to Agent Orange in Vietnam exacerbated. The VA considers his death to be "service connected" because of that exposure and the known effects that have been proven with Agent Orange exposure and diabetes. In 2014 he was in a bicycle accident and suffered a serious TBI (Traumatic Brain Injury) from which he never fully recovered. In 2017 he fell and broke his hip, which devastated him even further. Then in 2018 he suffered two strokes (related to diabetes) that left his brain scrambled. In the end he stopped eating, which was the real cause of his death. He chose to leave because he couldn't deal with all the damage his brain had endured. It was his choice. It was extremely sad and a very difficult decision, but it was ultimately his to make. He took control of the only thing he could control. I stood by him and advocated for his wishes.

A few days after his passing, we had a Celebration of Life Memorial. Here is the eulogy I wrote for his service.

Eulogy

A lot of you knew Jeff before this bike crash and TBI. And many of you only know Jeff after his bike crash and TBI. There is quite a difference between the two. However, there was one part of Jeff that never changed and that was his genuineness - he was just as he seemed in so many ways. There was never anything pretentious about Jeff, he was authentic through and through. He was a kind, gentle, honest, deep thinking, soul, who loved to help people. However, there was a side he kept private, a side filled with pain, suffering, regrets, and unending memories of the horrors of war.

I met Jeff 34 years ago. Our first conversation on the phone lasted two hours. We connected quickly and deeply. From that moment on we have been together. Our life has had many ups and down and lots of trials and tribulations, but something always held us together. We had a bond that was deep, and we both felt like we may have known each other in other lifetimes. It was one of those relationships. We "got" each other and were connected at a soul level. We both felt like the "black sheep" of our families and in life. We were a matched set, traveling companions through the crazy experience of life. We had big lessons to learn from each other and learning them was often frustrating and many times exasperating, but in the end we both grew deeper in our own truth and understanding of our histories and our wounds.

We both had lots of wounds. Unfortunately, the one deep wound that linked us was the effects of war. I was raised by a WWII combat Marine who suffered from "shell shock". He taught me to stand at attention and sing the Marine Corps hymn by the time I was three. He was tortured by nightmares and bouts of malaria. He was haunted by the memories of battles and survival. He was lauded as a hero for killing over 200 Japanese in Saipan. (Something he never wanted my brother or I to know. We found that out after he died.)

When I met Jeff, there was an immediate connection. What I didn't know then, but understand now, is that we were drawn towards each other by our war wounds. Me, being raised in a home filled with fear by someone with raging PTSD, and Jeff, the gentle soul, trying to navigate life after Vietnam, pretending to live a normal life, but haunted with memories, nightmares and flashbacks.

Jeff was drafted before he graduated from high school in 1966. He joined the Marines in hopes of getting the best training, not realizing he just increased his chances of being in combat exponentially.

Jeff fought in some the biggest battles of the war, the first wave. The Battle for Hue and the Ten Offensive, the biggest and bloodiest battles of the war. What those 13 months "in country" did to an innocent boy from Akron, Ohio, who had never been out of the state prior to enlisting, can never fully be comprehended. But the impact it made, turned Jeff into another person. The Jeff that left Ohio for bootcamp, never returned.

I have a philosophy about Jeff. I call it "all roads lead to Vietnam." No matter where he went, who he was with, or what the circumstances, within minutes he was talking about Vietnam. It defined him, haunted him, and isolated him. He collected books and memorabilia about the war, he watched every documentary and movie made about Vietnam. In his early years home, he loved to argue war politics with anyone who would listen. He became a survivalist and had elaborate plans "incase" of an invasion or attack. He collected guns, knives, and gadgets and became a "MacGyver" of survival.

With the help of counseling at the Vet Center, on several occasions, Jeff could gain some ground in the battle with Vietnam, but in time would slip back into his old patterns. There were nightmares, and hypervigilance, and startle response issues. Plus, the ongoing internal suffering he blocked out by watching violent movies or using his body to the limit riding motorcycles and then bicycles, seeking adrenaline rush. Vietnam and the effects of war never left us. It was part of our life.

While preparing for his Celebration of Life, I found some journals Jeff kept from early 2001. I had seen them before but never looked at them, respecting his privacy. Yesterday I started reading though them, what I found surprised me. He was honest, open and vulnerable. He shared his struggles and his hope. (I have included his writings, word-for-word in the next section.)

Let me begin by saying that Jeff was a deep thinker. After Vietnam he wanted to understand the "why" of it all and read a lot. He read political books on the war, history books, and eventually moved into philosophy and spiritual books. He was greatly influenced by Buddhism, something that affected him deeply while in country. He connected with it and it was something he held on to for a small sense of peace.

Here is a quote he had written in the front of his notebook:

"The concept of scarcity only exists in a limited framework of a static reality. In a dynamic framework of infinite possibilities, we only need to reconceptualize reality to see any outcome we want and set our mind to it."

This is the type of quote he would read to me often and we would discuss. He was always looking fo r a way to understand and *conquer the mental conditioning he experienced in war and the pain it caused.*

In 2001 we applied for VA Disability for Jeff's PTSD. He was denied and we had to file an appeal and fight it. Thankfully, he won and was finally compensated. It took nearly 4 years. For the application process he had to write a "stress letter" describing the incidents that he felt contributed to his PTSD. He wanted to share this letter with his family, especially his son Scott. I'm not sure that ever happened. Writing about these experiences he felt would help his family better understand what happened to him and why it has been so difficult for him to overcome. (I have included that letter at the end, for a better understanding of what he experienced.)

In 2010 we moved back to California to be near my ailing parents. Jeff loved the weather and started cycling again. He met a great group of older riders, his first real friends in years. They rode several times a week and hiked on the weekends. He seemed to be enjoying life, although Vietnam was never too far away, it seems that he had turned a corner and was relatively happy.

Then on September 1, 2014, nearly 4 years ago, Jeff went out for a Monday ride with his buddies and a simple mistake caused a major crash and Jeff suffered a Traumatic Brain Injury (TBI). He was life flighted to Arrowhead Hospital Neuro Trauma Center.

Within the days that followed it was clear that we were dealing with a different Jeff. The brain injury had caused some major damage, but no one could tell us how long it would take for him to return to "normal" or if he ever would. The favorite phrase of his neurologist

was "No two brain injuries are alike." So, Jeff was sent home, orders for physical therapy, speech therapy and a suggestion to join a support group with other TBI survivors at the VA. We were both feeling helpless, confessed and unprepared for recovery.

In the days and weeks that followed I began to see a different Jeff. It seemed he was more light-hearted and carefree. He laughed more and seemed almost childlike. He asked to eat some bacon. I was shocked because he had been a vegetarian for nearly 40 years, and I had never seen him eat meat. He loved the bacon, and I remember so clearly the look on his face and him asking me "Now, why is it that I don't eat meat?" I laughed and tried to explain what he had told be previously. He shook his head and said, "Bacon is the best thing I had ever tasted."

Next, I realized that he seemed to have lost his issues with Vietnam. Things were different. He started telling me stories of his childhood that I had never heard before. It was like Vietnam was knocked out of the way and he could go back in time and remember what he loved about being a kid. It felt like a miracle! After nearly 30 years together I was hearing stories about his life that allowed me to see a whole new Jeff. A fun loving, interested, connected person who had dreams and goals for a future. Dreams and goals that were halted by a draft notice.

One day I came into the living room and all around him on the floor were guns and rifles. He had been an avid gun collector and had owned a gun shop many years ago. Honestly, I had never seen them all together before. He was usually very diligent about keeping them locked up and hidden. I asked him what he was doing. He said "I am taking all the firing mechanisms out of these guns. I couldn't live with myself if any of these were stolen and someone was killed with one of these guns. I'm making them unfireable."

Jeff used to be an expert with firearms, but as I watched him take the guns apart and throw the parts into a box, I was wondering if in his new mental state, he really knew what he was doing and if these guns would ever go back together again.

What I didn't know then, but soon came to realize was that Jeff had lost his survival personality, the one that was an adaptation to the trauma he experienced and the one he created for emotional and spiritual survival during his time in Vietnam. His macho, tough guy Marine was gone and in its place was 10-year-old Jeff. A sweet, kind, gentle spirit that loved people, life, animals, nature. It was hard for me to get my head around this new Jeff.

One day he told me a story about his 12th birthday. His dad had given him a pellet rifle. He was thrilled, it was his first "real" gun. He took it to his bedroom in the attic and took aim out a window and sighted in a cardinal sitting on a branch of a big tree in the back yard. He watched the bird and sighted in again and took the shot. The little red cardinal dropped off the branch and fell to the ground dead. He told me that was the worst feeling he ever had. If he could take it back, he would in a heartbeat. He said that was the last time he ever killed a living thing and knew he could never be a hunter. All that changed in 1966 . . . he got his draft notice and chose to join the US Marines and he went to Vietnam as a trained killer.

The story really impacted me, the way he told it, like a little kid and with such feeling. Taking the life of a small little bird and how it impacted him, understanding that life was so fragile. It showed me, what I already knew about Jeff, that he was an extremely, gentle spirit. That killing was not in him.

At first, I was happy for him because he seemed free in a sense. He started painting! Yes, I said that right, painting with acrylics. I was flabbergasted. This was definitely a new Jeff.

Jeff with two of his paintings in the Center for Spiritual Living Art Show.

But as time progressed, I began to see what the shift really meant. The horror of Vietnam had left him, the memory of the battles and the gruesome images and smells, the anger and the distrust of our government. That was nearly gone, but what replaced it was his pain, shame, and inability to come to terms with the fact that he had killed people. It had grown huge in his mind and he couldn't let it go.

For the next couple of years as he worked on his recovery from the TBI he fluctuated between being a happy go lucky 10-year-old and a sad, remorsefully man who was forced to fight in a war that didn't make sense to him and kill people who he saw as, "Just trying to live their lives."

We talked about forgiveness and letting go, but he couldn't. The TBI gave him freedom in one way, and in another created a deeper pain. At church, every service would remind him in one way or another how it was impossible for him to forgive himself for what he had done. No matter what we told him, he just couldn't let it go. I think that is what started his marathon movie watching - it was his escape from that reality. With his headphones on, the screen in his lap, he could escape into a fantasy world where he could forget. It worked for him. Until it didn't anymore.

There are only a few people here today who know the old Jeff. Those are his sisters. They grew up with him and saw him grow into a young man. They knew their brother and loved the guy he was. He played with them, and listened, he looked out for all his brothers and sisters, he helped neighbors rack leaves and shovel snow, he babysat, and worked on cars, he played ball in the street with the neighborhood kids. He loved to eat his mom's fresh homegrown tomatoes. He was in love with the girl across the street and was trying to figure out a way to get to third base with her. When he got his draft notice, months before high school graduation he had to get an encyclopedia to look up Vietnam and figure out where it was in the world. The encyclopedia was old and in it the area was still referred to as "Indo China." His room in Akron, Ohio it seemed a lifetime away from a war being fought thousands of miles away in a foreign country.

Jeff's sisters, Debbie, Sandy and Kathy are the last to know the "old" Jeff. Because the "old" Jeff died in Vietnam. The Jeff that returned was nearly a stranger, and he was never the same again.

Of course, the basic nature of Jeff couldn't be killed, but it was dimmed so much that at times it was hard to see. but occasionally he broke free and allowed himself to be his naturally silly, comedic self - which we all loved and would eat up! And, of course, he loved the attention.

Over the past few weeks, as we watched Jeff fading away, he still talked about Vietnam. I sat with him and we talked about forgiveness and letting go. We talked about how young he had been and that he really had no choice. I reminded him of what a good person he is and told stories of things he had done for people. We laughed as we remembered, but he couldn't buy it. No matter how good he was to anyone, it wasn't enough to take away the damage that killing people had done to him. He just couldn't allow that level of self-forgiveness.

Jeff intentionally ended his life. He stopped eating. He knew the end result. I asked him "You know what's going to happen if you stop eating." He said, "Yes, I'll die." That was a very hard thing to hear. And an even harder thing to support and witness.

The pain of the past four years, the bike crash, the broken hip, the strokes, his memory issues (He kept telling me his mind was crazy), along with his guilt and inability to forgive himself for what he had to do in Vietnam pushed him into that decision.

Jeff didn't want a military funeral. He wanted to be remembered for himself. A kind, gentle, loving spirit with a wicked sense of humor, a generous soul. He was the most accepting and non-judgmental person that I had ever known. He was a sage and a wiseman. And his most profound and meaningful traits were his honesty and authenticity.

I won't be saying goodbye to Jeff, because he will always be with me. There were times when we could read each-others thoughts. He is part of me, and I am part of him. That kind of connection can never be broken. We loved each other oddly, but deeply, we knew that our connection lived beyond this world and the third dimension!

Where-ever he is now I wish him the peace he couldn't find in this life.

Just days before he died, we talked about finding each other in our next lives. He suggested in our next life we get a boat and travel the world. I laughed and told him I was afraid of the ocean, and he said, "Don't worry we'll work it out". We both laughed at that because it was something we both believed fully.

Yes, Jeff we all ways do!

Jeff and I talked often about how wonderful it would be to never have conflicts or war. Our wish for the world is to find a way to peace, so that no one will ever suffer the deeply damaging wounds of war that Jeff had to endure.

I want to end with a quote I read to Jeff just a few days ago from a book written by a Vietnam combat Marine called: "What It Is Like To Go To War" by Karl Marlantes. I got his attention, and as he looked me in my eyes, I read the quote.

"A nation that makes a great distinction between its scholars and its warriors will have its thinking done by cowards and its fighting done by fools." - Spartan King, quoted by Thucydides

Jeff looked away for a minute, then turned back to be with a grin and said, "That's a good one!"

Jeff was no fool. He was just an innocent young man from Akron, Ohio, stepping up to serve his country as men in his family had done before him. What he didn't expect was to have that service define and haunt him for the rest of his life.

I love you, Jeff.

May the peace you couldn't find in life be yours now.

The Journal

For many, many years I facilitated a 13-week class based on the book *The Artist's Way*, by Julia Cameron. Over the years, Jeff and I would run into people around town (in Akron) who had taken the class when we were out and about. I would chat with them and when we walked away, he would say, "Artist's Way?" and I'd nod. Never in all the years that I taught it did I ever expect Jeff to take the class. So, when he said he thought he'd like to be in the next class I was blown away. A friend of his from church had signed up to take it and urged him to join. So, he did. As part of the process, he'd have to write something called "morning pages". Three pages of writing first thing in the morning. Basically, stream of consciousness writing. Every day for 13 weeks. That is a big ask. And for Jeff to sign up for that, it was really big. Huge!

He saved those *Artist's Way* journals and they were always included in his important "stuff" box he kept in the closet. I never read them. I only knew what he shared with me in conversations.

As I was preparing for his Celebration of Life, I looked in that box for one of his spiritual books so I could use a quote and I saw his *Artist's Way* journals – they were two small-sized spiral notebooks. I took them out and decided to read them. I was surprised by what I read. It moved me to see how seriously he took it, had open and vulnerable he made himself, and in it he clearly described the war demons he was always fighting. I realized how much he had grown, how all the spiritual books he had been reading had impacted him, and how much he wanted to have his story told.

Following is the transcript of his "morning pages". This is the word-for-word transcription, nothing left out. I don't feel this is a betrayal, even though he said numerous times "no one will be reading this." What I believe is this is Jeff's way of leaving a piece of him behind to tell some of his story in his own words.

Jeff's Morning Pages Journal 2001

10-15-01

Well, here I am it's my first day of the Artist's Way morning pages. I have high hopes of gaining some insights into myself from this class. My biggest worry is that I will stop along the way because it's too hard or I get lazy. That seems to be my pattern. I start out good and then slow down and pretty soon I can't find the time, so I put it off till the next day. I thought that writing three pages a day would be very hard for me but thanks to my Summer Institute class I knew I could do it.

This morning writing to clear your mind, I hope it works as good as Julia says it does. I think I'm going to count the words I write when I get done and see how many there are. It's hard to write on the back side of the page the big spiral gets in the way. This seems like babbling to me. I want to try to think of something witty to say even though I know this is supposed to be free flowing out of my mind. I find myself avoiding words that I am unsure of how to spell. This is probably something I should look at later on. There seems to be a lot of distraction – the dog wants to go out and pee. There are big trucks going by now, the dog is barking at something. Maybe I should think about getting up earlier so it will be more quiet and less distracting for me. Well, I'm out of space and there's a garbage truck outside drawing my attention away from my work. Although this seems like it might be fun when I get the hang of it. I have written three and one-half pages already. Bye for now. Jeff

10-16-01

Day 2 Woke up at 2:57 am last night never really got back to sleep. I don't like writing on the backside of these pages but it would be a waste to leave them blank? Maybe I will buy a new writing instrument today. Something that costs a lot to remind me that this class is important to my growth. Need to finish my cover soon and do the contract. Would remind myself in these pages but I am not supposed to read back on them. Ha Ha. I will just remember on my own. This war thing has really got me depressed. I am so glad Scott is too old to be drafted. Don't think they will bring the draft back anyway, but I still worry for all the young men and everybody else too. I must read my chapter sometime today. Think I might take the book with me and stop somewhere and take time to read it. I need to make this a priority.

The thoughts are coming too fast in my mind to write down. Guess this is a good thing. Shouldn't worry so much about the spelling. I'm the only one who is going to read this anyway. Gave up on punctuation before I started. I will throw in a period now and then just because three pages of this size is too short. Will use bigger book next time. Bye for now. Jeff

10-17-01

Here I am writing with my new pencil and it writes nicely. I'm worried about getting back to Fairlawn to finish up my work there. It seems silly but that the way I feel. I suppose I should take a look at why I am so insecure about what I do for them. I need to think more positively and let the Universe take care of the plan for me. Control over life is an illusion.

Our money situation seems okay. I need to let that go as well. Everything is going to be alright as long as I keep trusting in the Universe and keeping a positive attitude. I am worried about my spelling again, which is stupid. No one but me is going to read this. I need more positive self-talk about myself. This is turning out to be a very negative three pages. I wonder why? Now I am very self-conscious about the way I'm feeling this morning. Maybe this is all part of the process of doing Morning Pages. Now I know why Julia thinks it's a good idea to read the chapter right away when the week starts. Time flies, here it is Wednesday and I still haven't read the chapter. Must get to it today. There are tasks to complete which will take time and time is running out. Bye for now. Jeff

10-18-01

Don't feel like writing today. Thinking about work and breakfast. Like my new pencil. Still can't stop worrying about spelling. Still haven't read the chapter. Need to be billings. Need to get truck fixed. Need to get started earlier. Need to stop eating ice cream. It makes me feel bad afterwards. May be part of the reason I can't sleep good, but I think it has more to do with the war than anything else. Can't seem to shake the feeling of doom that hangs over me. Need to think more positive and believe in the Universe.

Well, I'm glad I got all that down on paper. Had no idea that there was that much going on in my head. I think I feel a little better already. It's a wonderful Fall day outside. I need to get outside and enjoy it while I can. Maybe I won't have to work all day today and I can go somewhere and read my chapter this week before it's over. I know there are tasks to complete. Don't want to screw up on. My first week of the book. Bye for now. Jeff

10-29-01

Well, I'm back. Still don't like writing on this back page. Made the connection in group yesterday that this has to be a priority for me. I always have the tendency to let the work on myself go. Still thinking about spelling, which leads me back to school in my younger days. I can remember being worried all the time about looking stupid. Thought everyone was waiting for me to screw up so they could laugh at me. I am at least remembering my childhood even if I have to start with bad memories. I can't think of anything else to write about that strikes my fancy. Think I will just write whatever comes to mind. Must read my chapter today and get started on my homework. I don't think it will be hard to do. I really need to start exercising and get some strength back into my left shoulder. It is healed well enough now so I can start maybe when I get the garage cleaned out. I can make a little workout area in there. Get the weights out and get my bike up on the trainer and get a jump on spring this winter. Well, that's enough for now. Bye. Talk to me later. Jeff

10-30-01

Trying to distract myself this morning, didn't want to get started. Cindy says when you look back after 6 weeks you can see patterns form. We'll see. Vaguely worried about new terrorist attack. Must remember that control of any situation is an illusion. Must live day to day and enjoy the good things that the Universe brings to me. There is always good and bad going on at the same time. It's which one that you choose to focus on that you see, and the more good and happiness you look for, the more you will find and then I will be a force for good and a light for others. I'm starting to sound like Gary (He was reading Gary Zukav, The Seat of the Soul) That's a good thing.

Think I will try to talk to my sisters and brother about all this when I see them in December. It's not too far off now. I need to get my truck fixed soon. Wish my checks would get here, they will probably today or tomorrow. Think this writing thing in the mornings helps you get a good start on the day. I think I will try to write one positive thing in here each day to start me off on a good note. Well, time to go. Talk to you in the morning. Jeff

10-31-01

Well, here I am again. The dog is bothering me because I have food. I am thinking about my day and if I will have anything to do. Today I am worried that my blood sugar is up. Because of my weight and not exercising. Must start a program soon. I know I'll feel better if I start. My back could even get better. Think I'll talk to Doctor Rod about my back when I see him. I think maybe I'm getting old, complaining about aches and pains. Lucky, no procedures or operations yet. Ha Ha (A nod to the movie City Slickers) Well, it's really nice day outside. I think I will read the rest of the chapter and go down by the lake today if I have no pressing work to do. Must go see Greg today before I forget to give him a bill. Need to get on top of this bill thing. Hope I get my check today, have very little money to spend, don't like it like this. Need to go to Al and Bee Lashers, as well. They need me. Must call Linda Gannon too. So, I guess I have plenty to do if I want to get down to it. Well enough for now. Jeff

11-1-01

Another nice fall day outside. Sun shining, warm for fall. I finished my chapter and the part about making positive affirmation is what I need and saying something good about myself and the day. Every day in these pages I already talked about the nice day and the cool looking leaves, Now, for me – I am a good person and people like me and I am a good speller. I'm going to try the spelling thing and see how it works. I need to write what I want and not have to use words that I can spell instead of words that are hard for me to spell. Well, that is enough of that today. I am going down to the lake and do my homework for the class. It's already Thursday. Got to get going on it. Wonder if we will have a hard winter this year? Hope it is short. I really don't like getting cold. Need to buy those gloves at Marc's before they are all gone. Shirts and socks too. Oh, I just had a good idea. I could ride my bike down to the lake with my notebook and book and get in some sight-seeing, exercising, and home work all at one time. I think that's what I'll do. Need to start taking my vitamins, especially C and E. Well, that's it for now. Jeff

11-4-01

Well, it's been two days since I did my Morning Pages, but I don't feel guilty about it. I'm not into that any more. All the money problems are under control. There is no need to get all depressed about it. Just move on and do what you know you should be doing anyway. Pay attention to what you are doing and why. Well, it's a beautiful day outside. I need to make time before it gets too cold to go for a long walk on the Tow Path and see the leaves. Will start to clean out the garage this week so I can set-up my work out area and get started on my come back. I feel it coming on.

This is the start of the season for my PTSD. This year I'm not going to let it creep up on me and put me in a funk – stay ahead of it and work it out by talking about it. Maybe I'll give my book to Marilyn to read and talk to her about some of it. Well enough for now. Jeff

11-5-01

Well, had some excitement this morning. Lucy (a dog from down the street) came to play with Millie. They ran around for a half hour or so then I took Lucy back home. I left our phone number in case they want to get rid of her. We will take her in a minute! She and Millie get along really well. I will try to clean out the garage today if I don't have any work to do. I am going to get my workout area in shape and maybe build some more storage areas. Can't think of much to write about today. Slept good last night, not so worried as before. Wonder what will happen next on the war front? Barb's talk was very good yesterday. Hope the UUA topic of Globalization takes hold with the congregation. Would be nice to get into something meaningful that could change history for the betterment of the whole planet. Very lofty idea, but I think it could be the key if only man could stop his greed for things and power. Seems hopeless, but we need to try. It's the right thing to do. Well, off the soap box for now. Jeff

11-6-01

Vet Group today. I wonder if the guys will show up or not? Had a good night's sleep even though I watched that show "Uprising". Not sure what that means, have to wait a few more days to see if I have a bad reaction or not. I feel pretty good now that I have made up my mind to stay on top of my trigger time of year. Must come up with a plan to take care of myself to counter act the depression. Exercise has to be a key component. Hope my trip to Wade Park (VA facility in Cleveland) is good and I get on the registers and get something. We could really use the money. I guess I should not look at it that way but can't help it. Well, whatever. Had a dream about the old neighborhood last night. It was kind of comforting to go back to the old days when things seemed so much simpler and innocent back then. Maybe that's what I slept so good. The dog is bugging me so I have to hurry. Got to go to group. Jeff

11-7-01

Kind of disappointed that the VA backed my appointment up until January, but no big deal. Gives me time to get my truck fixed before going to Cleveland. Keep thinking about exercise and my weight and sugar. Need to get started soon. Have to work on the garage. Need to write note and call Linda Cannon for tomorrow to work. I have to go on an Artist's Date and start my list of 21 things I enjoy. Maybe I will get the basketball out and go shoot some hoops. Haven't done that in a long time. May ride my bike before the weather turns bad or go to the movies. That would also be fun. Have to start holiday gifts soon. Need to make something for Elisha, Jen and Cindy. Maybe a necklace or earrings or something for Jen's house. I'm thinking too much and not just writing. Well, I'm distracted. Enough for today. Jeff

11-8-01

Here I am and can't think of anything to write. Must do my Artist's Date today. I will go on a ride to the lake at Szalay's, take my book and hang out. It's going to be warm today and sunny all day, I hope! Seem to be having a block on what to write so I'm going to try to just write whatever comes to mind. Well, nothing is coming to mind so I'll write that and just keep writing. Maybe this is what Julia was talking about that some days would be hard and you just have to keep going and stick with it.

Well, two pages down, one to go. No brain storms yet. I'm thinking about my flashlight project and the switch. Maybe I don't have it in me to get whatever I'm supposed to get out of this exercise. It does clear my head for the day and gives me a chance to look out the window. I like looking and being outdoors when it's nice. Well, I made it! Jeff

11-10-01

Well, it's the day after the big car wreck. We were very lucky. Once again, can't help but think that the Universe is looking out for us. With all the cars and trucks that were around that intersection and all moving at 30 to 40 MPH. It's a wonder more people were not hurt. I thank God or whatever anyone wants to call him or her or it or whatever that he is looking out for us and guiding me through my travels on this wonderful journey I call my life. He has always been there for me and even though I don't understand what he is trying to show me at the time that it's happening, I can look back now and finally at age 54 I am beginning to understand what life is all about and why I need to appreciate every day we are given. All the things that happen to us, even when we don't understand them and we think they are hurting us. Those times are the biggest lessons for us if we will just stop and look at what is important here and now everyday as it comes. That's all you get and that's all you need to get, once you figure it out. Very profound of me, I think this must be one of those light bulb moments, you know, clarity. Well enough for today. I am going to enjoy my day, my coffee, and the fall season outside and thank God I'm alive. Jeff

11-12-01

Monday. Two days after Chuck the dog came to our house. He seems nice, but he is a male and he and Millie are still working out who is the boss. We will see if he gets to stay or not.

We are low on money again, but I am turning it over to the Universe and asking for help every day. Things will work out for the best. I know it! I made it through the Marine Corp's birthday and Veteran's Day. I think I'm doing okay, but sometimes I'm not the best judge of the situation. I'm sure Cindy will let me know if I'm getting too depressed. The holidays will be here soon and for the first time in a long time I'm kind of looking forward to seeing everyone and how they are doing. Thinking in bed this morning how short a time that I lived on Chalker Street. In my memory it seemed so long, most of my childhood, yet it was only 7 ½ years. At that point I guess it was half of my life and all of my experience so that why it had so profound of an effect on me and the rest of my life. Well, bye for now. Jeff

11-14-01

The dogs are here bugging me as I write. They are cute together, one so big, the other so small. Wish we could keep both, but I guess not. Need to get some work done, clean up these little jobs that are half done. Pretty soon Kosmic Korners will be calling all over the place and I'll have no time for anything else.

I'm going on my Artist's Date today and work on my tasks. It will only be an hour or two down to the pond and ride on my bike and maybe a movie. I have to do Billings and get them in the mail. I wonder what it would be like to have your kids living around you all the time and coming by to see you all the time with their kids. Hope

that happens to us at some point soon. I'll put that out to the Universe and expect to get some good feedback real soon. A little girl and boy would be nice. Another great day today. I guess I'll go out and enjoy it. That's enough for now. Jeff

11-15-01

Got my billings done yesterday. I did my Artist's Date, sort of. I think I need to do another one just because it's so nice out. I want to ride my bike and at least start to clean the garage. Maybe if I do a little bit at a time it won't seem so overwhelming. I'm worried about my weight and sugar. I think I'll check it more often than I have been. I still want to go to the show, maybe today or tomorrow. I should get a spell check here at the desk, but that would stop the stream of consciousness writing and spoil the whole reason for this exercise.

The dogs seem to be getting along much better. Maybe we will keep Chuck. Well, can't think of anything else to write now. I wonder how the war is going and that makes me think about the trip to see The Wall and all the work on pain that must be done before we go. I hope the other guys are willing to give it a try. I think it would do me some good, but my stomach hurts now just thinking about it. That means there is still a lot going on about that for me. Well, enough for now. Jeff

11-16-01

Well, and interesting night last night and a strange morning so far. Kent, the drunk that lives above us, kept us up last night with noise so the dogs barked for an hour or so at 3:30 am. Then he's up making noise early this morning. Well, I stood up for myself and complained to Peggy and Jerry (the apartment managers). They called and read him the riot act. Makes me feel good about the fact I stood up for myself. I must be getting better. I didn't even have to think about it, I just did it.

I think Chuck is settling in nicely. Hope he can stay. He and Millie seem to be getting along fine now. Hope this thing with Barb and Marilyn works itself out without to much more trouble. We don't need this kind of bad karma in our lives right now. Got to go, more later. Jeff

11-17-01

My blood sugar is down to 127 which is pretty good. I think it has to do with the volume of food, as much as what kind of food. At least I'm glad it is on the way down. I really need to watch it.

Another week almost gone by, still no bike ride. I'm just going to keep writing about it till I do it and not feel bad about it.

Thinking about my family and the holiday. We don't have a lot in common but I love them and want to see them. We can have fun for a while. Hope they don't ask how I'm doing too much, they might get more than they want to hear. I guess I owe them some kind of explanation. Guess I'll have to deal with it when I get there. Not going to worry about the future, try to stay focused on the present. As they say, that's all I really have anyway. Bye for now. Jeff

11-18-01

Not much time before church. Another beautiful day outside. Maybe today I can go for a bike ride. I'm satisfied with my eating and my sugar is better. I need to keep this weight off and lose some more. It really makes a big difference in my sugar and I can still eat what I want, just keep from eating too much at a sitting.

Well, got some of the paperwork done for my PTSD. Hope something good comes out of it. I know something good will come out of it, the Universe will provide for me, I just need to keep working on myself. Bye for now. Jeff

11-19-01

Monday contacting VA about Agent Orange. Today Cindy's sending off the financial statement to get more compensation. I still have mixed feelings about all this even after all this time. I'm still waiting for my diabetes testing or blood testing or what ever it is. The people are really nice, but the whole setting bothers me.

Well, I'm going to make Pecan Tarts. I need at least 100. It will be fun to have everybody over and cook all the food and talk. I wish all my family lived closer and we could meet on holidays like the old days. At least I have those good memories to think back on. Lots of people don't even have that. All they remember is drinking and fighting and bad times. Funny how people can't even get along for a few hours one day a year. Sad, very sad. Well, we are going to have a nice sober holiday with no fighting.

I am still thinking about the PTSD Trauma Processing group. We are thinking of getting started on it. It will be very interesting to see who is willing to work and who is not and how deeply we can get into it. The sand box thing seems like a very good idea. We will talk more about it on Tuesday I hope. Bye for now. Jeff

11-20-01

Tuesday. Group day at the Vet Center. Hope all the guys show up. Today I could use an uplift. My spirts are lagging today. It's very cold out but bright and sunny. I feel physically okay, but kind of down in the dumps. I am going to keep a positive mind set on money. I know that the Universe will bring abundance to me so I refuse to worry about it. Everything is going to work out fine. We will have a lovely holiday at Thanksgiving and Winter Solstice. It will be great. Then we can start a new year off right.

Well, it didn't take as long to write three pages as I thought and they are up beat and positive so that bodes well for the rest of the day. I'm going to get a good cup of joe at Angel Falls and start the day off on a good note. Bye for now. Jeff

11-21-01

Another bright, sunny day outside. Sitting here by the window every day is a treat that I never thought of before when I was in a big hurry to start my day and go to work. This taking time for yourself is a very good thing. I now am thinking of maybe trying to work in a walk in the woods two or three times a week. Here it is Wednesday and I have not even thought about my Artist's Date yet. If I put it off until after Thanksgiving when everyone is here I probably won't do it at all and then feel guilty about it. Well, I still need to do the chapter as well so I better get started soon.

I'm thinking of abundance at night before I go to sleep and writing about it in my Morning Pages so I expect it.

11-22-01

Here it is Thanksgiving and I have a lot to be thankful for. Yesterday there was a woman on Oprah who taught Oprah to keep a gratitude journal. I think I'm going to do at least one thing I'm grateful for each day in this book, but today I'm grateful for having my family here for Thanksgiving. I'm grateful for Chuck so Mille has someone to play with.

It's another beautiful day outside. We're going to have a great dinner at Jen's and Pecan Tarts and pie. My coffee is wonderful and I feel pretty good. Life is good, it doesn't get any better than this. Well, if my nightmares would go away all together that would be better. But, this year I think I'm on top of it and I'm not going to let them get the best of me. Bye for now. Jeff

11-23-01

Had a very nice Thanksgiving yesterday. Good food, good friends, good relatives, and Scott called me in the evening. A very nice day. Today is bright and sunny, clear. Looks like another perfect day. Went to sleep thinking about the abundance that is coming my way now.

The dogs are getting along well. They are very funny together. When they are playing Chuck seems to have more energy now that he has been getting regular meals. He is so laid back most of the time. Well, will be going to church soon to see the guys and talk about Buy Nothing Day. Will have a good time if people show up. We will have good food regardless.

I've got to clean out the garage in the back soon so Jerry (the manager) can park his truck back there. Will be interesting to see if he really will or they just want my stuff out of the garage. That's all for now. Jeff

11-25-01

The big blow up came last night and it was the mother of all fights. I guess I should have expected it but it kind of caught me off guard. I thought everyone was getting along okay, but I guess that was an illusion, like so much in life. People don't show their true feelings and find it hard to get along with others. It seems petty to me, some of the issues, but they are very hurtful to others. I've seen a side of Elisha that is not very nice. I know she is in pain and very confused about her life and part of all this is her trying to lash out at that pain. I hope that she can find her way to some help soon and sort all this out. Enough for now. Jeff

11-26-01

Everyone has gone home and the holiday is over. We are getting back to normal. It's another great day. I'm grateful for the sun and the warm temps. I'm starting to look forward to Winter Solstice at Barbs it should be fun. I think I'm going to try and go on a ride with Greg somewhere. We can get back into shape together. Got all my checks over the weekend and now all I have to do is go to the bank and face the music, so to speak. See how much it's going to cost me. I'm not going to let this happen again but I'm not going to beat myself about it either.

I'm grateful for the shape I'm in and the Universe is bringing great prosperity to me every day. I'm very lucky I discovered all this along the way, mostly the church and all of my good friends that support me and Cindy. Enough for now. Jeff

11-27-01

Have to hurry, got to go to group. Bad night's sleep last night again. Ever since the big blow up I've had war related nightmares. I'll bring it up in group today.

It's gray and rainy today. I'll see how my mood is if it changes from bright and sunny. I'm grateful for the insight I've gotten over the last few years. Maybe it is wisdom and not just information.

I expect to hear from the Universe any day now so I'm keeping my eyes peeled for anything that comes my way. I'm excited about it and am very grateful of what I have already received and not focusing on the small setbacks that have come my way. It truly is how you perceive the information and whether you focus on the positive or negative. Bye, Jeff

11-28-01

The smoke has cleared on the money thing and I have learned a very good lesson at the expense of only $200. The banks have a real racket going on overdraft and it only hurts the people who can't afford to get overdraft charges. Chalk another round up to the Corporate man. I won't be playing that game again.

It's cool and gray out, but not bad for the end of November. No snow yet and that's okay with me. Still not sleeping good and waking up tired. Hope this gets better soon. I'm tired of being tired. Ha ha. Maybe this money thing is the insight I needed to ask the Universe for help and get my life, at least about money, in order. I should know soon. I'm grateful for the information to think about.

The dog, the big one is barking in my ear and I'm trying to ignore her but it's hard when your ear drum is breaking. That's enough from here for now. Jeff

11-29-01

Another gray day. Running late today. Have to get out of here and go to work. I'm dropping weight, going back down to below 200. This time I'm going for 185 or lower. I have lost so much muscle mass that I need to be that light to get the fat off. I slept good last night even though I woke up a lot. I think the three Motrin's helped ease the aches and pains and let me rest some. I'm grateful for the work that gives me aches and pains, so it's good to work. I can slack up some when the Universe hooks me up with some more sustenance and I get ahead of the game. Whatever that game is! Well, I have to get out of here so this is enough for now. Jeff

11-30-01

Not much to report. Today the weather is still very warm. I, for one, like it that way and am very grateful to Mother Nature for the break we are getting this year. I can't tolerate the cold like I used to as a kid. I wouldn't mind if it didn't snow as long as that didn't upset the balance with unintended consequences. Man, I wish I could spell better, maybe I should get one of those kid spelling games and practice till I drill it into me.

I'm starting to think of all the way my life could be better now that the Universe is bringing me more prosperity. I will be more giving of my time and help people who are less fortunate than I am. Pay off bills, fix up my truck and give money to the church. Well, that's enough for now, got to get going. Jeff

12-1-01

December 1 and it's still warm out, no snow! Finally did an Artist's Date, went to the movies after work and before I came home. Then when I got home I found out we were going to the movies with Jen, so I saw two movies in one day! Good treat for me.

I'm grateful for my life and even more the ability to understand and appreciate all the good things I have and not dwell on the things I don't have. Irv Wetland and the Dali Lama say this is wisdom not just information. The insight to tell the difference is the key to a good life. There, I guess I figured out that one thing in life. That makes all that happens to one worth living through if one can look at it with the right perspective. Not so easy all the time but well worth the effort. In fact, it is the only tool one always has control of in their life always. Good page, I impressed myself. Jeff

12-2-01

Here it is Sunday and I've done my Morning Pages all week, gone on my Artist's Date, and worked on my chapter. Finally got it all together.

It's a bright, sunny day. Chilly, but not cold.

We had a great open house last night. Lots of our friends came over to see the art studio. It was very nice. We have a lot to be thankful for. My check came on time, all is right with the world. The Universe is providing us with a good life. Must remember to go by the VA and get a printout of my appointments on Tuesday after group. We need to get started on my appeal for PTSD. I really think I deserve more but I'll leave it up to the Universe to show me what is best and try to appreciate what I have already received which is a lot. Live in the moment!

Chuck is the perfect example of a gift. He is so good and loving and he just came to us out of the blue. Now Millie is better and they play together. Well, enough for now. Jeff

12-3-01

Another bright, sunny day in Akron, Ohio. So far this winter is okay with me. No snow, not too cold, and mostly dry. I'm going to the backpacking store with Greg. I need to get that knife I was thinking of for my sheath. I'll look at them at the store. I don't seem to have much to write today, don't know if that's a good thing or bad. Maybe I just don't have much on my mind to write about. Oh well, I'm not going to worry about it.

I'm grateful for my life and health. Speaking of which, maybe hiking the Towpath with a full pack can be part of my exercise plan to get back into shape. If the weathers bad it doesn't matter, you can always walk. I need to put this plan into action. Walk, then stop for lunch, make myself some soup. I need to dehydrate some veggies to supplement my soup mix when I find a good one. Enough for now. Jeff

12-4-01

Here it is December 4th already and it is still sunny and warm. This is so cool. I think that's why I'm in such a good mood. I think my open request to the Universe for more abundance has begun. I just have to keep an open mind and not question what is happening but accept it as the grace of God on me and be grateful for the bounty. The Universe works in strange ways. Kind of apprehensive about talking to Barb today but will remain upbeat and think thoughts create reality.

I have a good life and it is just getting better each day. I feel better in my stomach when I write it or say it. What you think and believe creates your reality. How simple to make your life better with just the way you look at your life. Da. Well, enough for today. Keep smiling. Jeff

12-5-01

Another great day. Sun is shining bright. The high today is going to be 68. I don't remember a day in December this warm, ever! Too bad my mom is gone I could ask her. I really miss everyone around this time of year and the good old days for family holidays. Oh well, I'm still going to make some Pecan Tarts and we will have some holiday cheer with our friends from church.

I'm so grateful for this new insight on the way to look positively on the things in your life that could be taken negatively and change the whole outcome. It gives one hope for the future. That's something I've not has since high school, before I went in the service. The Universe is beginning the cycle of prosperity and abundance, I can feel it happening. Not anything I can put my finger on, more like a feeling. I guess we will see soon enough. Now I've got to go to work. Write more later. Jeff

12-7-01

Friday. Still bright and sunny, not so warm as yesterday, but still very nice. Having a hard time with what to say this morning. I'm sleeping much better, but it's hard to get motivated for work. Think I'm sick, but not too sick yet to tell. Started popping vitamin C, 1000 milligrams to try to fight it off.

Went to see Harry Potter movie yesterday, very good. Reminds me to read the last book before the next one comes out. I really need to get my truck fixed so I can go to Cincinnati for the holiday. Better start thinking when to head back. If Christmas is on Tuesday, I get there on Wednesday, that would give me Thursday, Friday, Saturday, then come home on Sunday or Monday. That's what I'll do. I guess I need to think about it more, maybe play it by ear when I get there. It will be good to see everyone anyway. Enough for now. Jeff

12-17-01

I'm back after taking a week off. My plan of not letting the holidays get me down this year is not going so well. I feel numb and depressed at the same time. The only difference is I'm fully aware why thinking out a plan in your head and carrying it out in your heart are two very different things. I have tried to talk myself through this and use the tricks that I learned in group and the books I read, but I can't shake myself out of this funk I'm in. So now I'm going to try writing down what I feel good or bad and deal with whatever comes up. I'm very tired of trying to be upbeat during this time of year when that makes me feel guilty for living through all the fire fights and ambushes, not to mention the month in Hue, when so many men, better than me, died. It's very hard to deal with normal life back here in the world. It all seems so trivial.

I really don't see that I have much to complain about, I've got food to eat, a warm place to sleep and no one is looking to kill me just yet. In my head, I know I should want more, but in my heart I know I don't need or deserve more. What I need is to find meaning in the struggle for life, a reason to carry on that has meaning for me in my heart and up until now I just don't feel it and it's getting very hard to fake it. Well, this is getting very depressing so I think I'll stop for today and see how I feel tomorrow. Maybe this will give me some insight. I hope so. Jeff

12-19-01

I finally got my truck fixed. It was cheaper than they said, done faster that I thought and hardly a hassle at all. Proving that the Universe is looking out for me and I should not be so worried about things. They will always work out. I swear that when the days are brighter, so am I.

Talking about the holiday in my VA group on Tuesday really make me think back. I didn't say much, probably should have spoken up more, but didn't want to bring everyone down, so I kept it all to myself like I always do. Even though this season will be better than most, I hope that keeping myself busy will work pretty good. I'm still grateful for the progress I've made to this point though I think the trauma processing is going to have to happen. I just don't think that I can let it go until I can grieve that whole 13-month period. I must talk to Fran (VA therapist) and Dr. Shirley (VA Psychiatrist) about how to get started on some of this serious work. It keeps pulling at me and I keep trying to get away from it. Dr. Phil's little phrase "Walk away from your history and begin to write some new history", was very powerful for me the other day. I can't seem to get away from the feeling that I have. A heavy coat that I must wear all the time. Sometimes it feels like a warm friend in the winter, but most of the time it is a heavy burden that I never seem to be able to put away for the other seasons of my life. It keeps me from living the life I should be living and giving to the ones I love the care and attention they deserve from me. Well, enough for now. Jeff

12-21-01

Back to a bright, sunny day. It's cold outside, but no snow yet. Can't stop thinking about my trip to Cincinnati and whether to take my VA stuff or not. I'm not sure this is a good time of year to bring everyone down, but it's that time of year for me. Well, maybe I'll take it with me and see what happens. If they ask then I'll tell them all they want to know, but . . . Well NO buts. I feel I owe them that much. It may make them understand a little why I'm so different. Enough about that stuff. I don't want to bring myself down. I just wish I could get more motivated to find the joy in my life. It seems like my feelings in the crying and sadness area are much more alive, too alive. And my joy and happiness area are clipped off and *very short lived, when I let myself have them at all. I'm so into feeling guilty about being alive that my feeling bad about myself feels better than feeling good. More normal I guess or I relate to that part of me more readily. What's up with that? Well, I've got to go to the doctor at the VA at 10:20. It's almost 10:00 now so I'll end this for today. Jeff*

12 -24 -01

It's the night before Christmas and all though the house, well it's Christmas Eve and we are getting our first real snow of this year. It's almost 10:00 and the snows stopping now, but we've gotten an inch or so and everything is white. I'm glad it looks nice. Then I hope it goes away after Christmas. I feel pretty good so far. Keeping busy and staying with friends and even talking about it has helped. I'm looking forward to going to Kathy's and seeing everyone. I think it will be okay. Still worried about taking my paperwork and talking to everyone. Who knows when I'll have the chance to have everyone in one place again and be able to talk face to face. I feel I must take this opportunity to let everyone in on what is going on with my life so maybe they can gain some insight into me. I feel guilty about not giving them the whole picture of why I'm so weird sometimes. I think they all think I'm crazy or at least disturbed and I guess I am. I'm sure in the back of people's minds they wonder and somewhere they are afraid of me and somewhere in my own head I think they should be afraid. That makes me feel very sad. I never wanted to be one of those people that others are afraid of. Jeff

12-26-01

It's all over. Made it through another Christmas. Looking back, I have to say this might have been the most stress free one I've ever had. No big expectations, no big family gatherings, just a nice and quiet. We went to the show, saw a nice movie, came home and had a nice spaghetti dinner and talked to Jen and Marilyn. It was fun.

Now there's my family to deal with in Cincinnati. That's for another day. It's bright and sunny outside, kind of cold but it is December. I'm sleeping pretty good considering the intrusive thoughts happen more in the day time, but less than other years. So, I can deal with them easier and they don't seem to last as long. Still struggling with how to deal with this information I want to give my brother and sisters. I feel I must do something and I must trust that my gut is telling me the right thing to do and not be afraid of how it will come out. The Universe will take care of it. I just need to follow the path I know is layed out before me. I can no longer ignore this. Time is growing short. Jeff

12-28-01

Here I am, down at Kathy's. Everyone is here and having a good time and getting along well. It's good to see everybody. This is good. I think I could convert these people if we all lived closer together. Well, we are all on our own separate journey, so it's not my job to make sure everyone gets it. I am here for my own trip and I need to keep focused on that and trust that the Universe will bring us all to the right place in the long run. Sleeping alright. Still worried about the "stress letter" and how much to divulge. I would really like to know what they all really think and are too afraid to say.

It's much warmer down here than Akron and almost NO snow. Hope that Cindy is alright and that the dogs don't miss me as much as I miss them. Things here are getting hectic so I'll sign off for now. Jeff

1-7-02

We got about four inches of snow last night. Everything is white and really quite lovely. It's around 30 degrees, so not too cold for January standards.

Had a long talk last night with Jen and Cindy about my Morning Pages over the holidays. Some pretty heavy stuff for me. Didn't know I had that much pain behind this stuff that close to the surface. Seems like after all these years you think that it would subside, but it never does. I feel somewhat better about the whole thing now and don't feel so bad about not doing my Morning Pages or a week. Cindy brought that up to me, after bringing up all that pain it's no wonder I stopped. Funny how I fooled myself into thinking that it was just because I was lazy and didn't feel like writing. My mind can play tricks on me to avoid feeling the pain. I'm very lucky I have people around me that care enough to help me get through all this and give me insights that make me look at things differently. Well got to go for now. Going to try to be good to myself today. Jeff

1-9-02

I spoke up in group yesterday and I think we might start a trauma group and meet with Fran one on one to talk about the events that are always just under the surface for me. All and all late December and early January have given a lot of movement to my thought process. Kind of ironic because this is the time frame 30 years ago that got me in this situation. Leading into this season this year I was thinking about a plan to help me with the depression and here the Universe stepped in to help, which brings me back to my word for this year – TRUST. Trust in the Universe, trust in myself and trust in his journey I'm on even though I can't understand the way things are going sometimes. My best interest is always being looked out for. Someone or something is taking care of me. That is comfortable to realize. Jeff

1-10-02

Woke up today feeling tired and groggy and I think it was from the sugar in the ice cream I ate before I went to bed. Sugar is very bad for me. Must stop eating it. Still not exercising yet, but my weight is down. Keeping down the volume is the key to keeping the weight off.

I must do my Billings and get them in the mail. Don't know why I still do this, some sort of self-sabotage or something. I need to think about why I keep myself at this level of poverty. Maybe my upbringing or guilty feelings, not sure but it is a pain in the ass to always be behind on everything and trying to keep up. Still thinking about the drill set or the combo pack. You would think I would do something or let it go, but it's that same old thing I keep hanging on to it so I can have something to beat myself up with. Well this is getting depressing, so will end for now. Jeff

1-11-02

Thinking about my brothers and sisters today. Wonder if they read the letter and what they think of it and me. I need to call Sandy and find out if she got a copy from Kathy and I really should take one over to my brother's house. Maybe. Give it to Tippy and then he can read it when he gets home from work. That way he can call me if he has any questions. Well, enough about that. I wonder what talking to Dr. Shirley is going to be like. If she is interested or just going through the motions and what I'll say. Probably not too good to think too much about it before hand and just let come out whatever comes out. I think I'm going to take my Morning Pages with me just to push me on so I don't try to cover up because I'm too afraid to let it out. I think that is a good plan. Then Cindy can help me if I get stuck. Enough for now. Jeff

1-12-02

Saturday morning. Cold outside, but no snow. Don't have much to say today. Not much going on. Took a long time to get started today. Didn't feel much like writing. Still haven't done my Billings yet, can't seem to force myself to get into it. I hope spring comes early this year I'm already sick of winter already. Can't wait for spring. Still feeling the blues can't seem to make myself do anything. I have run out of things to say. I don't want to write anymore today. This is boring and seems very silly to me. How big can I write so as to fill up this page more quickly. Hope I am not blocked because this will be very hard to keep doing. Jeff

1-13-02

Still don't feel like writing. Not much on my mind. Had some weird dreams but can't remember them. It's bright and sunny out today which is good. Puts me in a better mood. Well I guess I need to hurry if we are going to go to church. It's 9:30 already. I hope my trip to Wade Park (VA) is useful tomorrow. I could use an uplift in mood and in money if you know what I mean. It sure would help. I am still putting my trust in the Universe despite what all the skeptics at VA are telling me. I think that guy doesn't know what he's talking about. Anyway, I made it through 3 pages after all so it may be getting better. Bye for now. Jeff

1-16-02

It's Wednesday. Talked to Fran in group. All I have to do is call the VA for an appointment to get started on the road to trauma processing. Sound like fun, Ha Ha. Well, I need to do it so fun or not.

Finally did my Billings yesterday. I'm not going to beat myself up about it. Just write it down for future reading and contemplation on my procrastination, which I think, is really a big stumbling block to my getting better more quickly. I really need to put some real work into what's behind all this unwillingness to do the work. I know it takes as long as it takes, but I need to keep pushing myself to get on with it. Well, I'm glad I've started tracking my blood pressure and sugar more often. It gives me peace of mind to know that I'm okay and that mean doctor was full of it. Ha Ha on her. Well enough of this for now. Time to go to work. Jeff

That was his last entry. Shortly after this, his VA therapist Fran and Dr. Shirley were activated to go to Iraq. They were part of a new attempt to help treat soldiers when they came out of action, before they went home, in order to minimize the effects of PTSD. Jeff was devastated. The work he was wanting to do on Trauma Processing was cancelled and their VA group trip to the Wall in DC was also cancelled. This was a setback he couldn't overcome. He tried to work with the new therapist and doctor that replaced Fran and Dr. Shirley, but it never jelled. He stopped going to group and never returned to the VA for therapy. This was a turning point for Jeff. He went into another downward spiral that lasted for years.

He never talked about trauma processing again. We did follow through with the compensation battle with the VA, and after four years of struggle he was finally awarded 100% disability based on his PTSD.

He still always wanted to go to the Wall but never made the trip. He talked about it all the time, and I suggested making plans on several occasions, but he wasn't ready. I don't know if he ever would have been. In July, after he passed, I took his story and some of his ashes to the Wall in DC and left them there. It was very emotional and heart wrenching, but it felt like closure for him.

With our daughter Elisha, and grandchildren Chealsea and Bella, we left a small jar of his remains, a heart charm, and a two-sided card with a small bit of his story along the Wall. It felt like the closure he had wanted for years. It was a deeply meaningful and emotional moment for me, knowing that I was completing his journey and paying tribute to him in a way not many people could truly understand.

Every evening, the Park Rangers gather all the notes, letters, pictures, and memorabilia and store them in the archives. One day they will all be on exhibit. His story will be included in the achieves. He would be happy.

Jeffrey T. Cochran

1947-2018

USMC

The soldier above all others prays for peace, for it is the soldier who must suffer and bear the deepest wounds and scars of war.

– Douglas MacArthur

Beloved husband, father, grandfather, brother, uncle. A kind and gentle spirit. May you finally be at peace.

Jeff Cochran USMC (Sgt. Jeffrey T. Cochran) 1947-2018

Died from complications to Agent Orange poisoning on May 30, 2018.

Jeff was born in Akron, Ohio and had never left the state. In his senior year of high school, just months before graduation, he received his draft notice. He had no idea where Vietnam was, so looked it up in an old encyclopedia. It might as well been on the moon. His world was so small, and he was so young, naïve, and inexperienced, that he decided to join the Marine Corp. He thought it would get the best training. But, instead, he was trained to fight in the first line. He was in the Tet Offensive and the Battle for Hue. That 19 year old, innocent boy from Ohio became a warrior. What he experienced in those 13 months "in country" changed him in ways that could never be repaired. In his 50's he was granted 100% disability for PTSD and Agent Orange Exposure. Vietnam effected every area of his life. Jeff was naturally a kind, gentle, loving man. What he had to do changed him, and haunted him until the day he died.

For years and years he wanted to come to DC to see the wall, but he never made it. Today we are bringing some of him here. May he Rest In Peace and finally be free from the nightmares, flashbacks and guilt that he could never overcome.

He was a beloved son, husband, father, grandfather, brother, uncle and friend.

Jeff, may your soul be free at last!

Vietnam Veterans Memorial

Vietnam War Memorial
"The Wall"
July 2018

NCENT P LANDON ·
UIZ · HOMER A RUPLE Jr ·
L SCHNEIDER · GAYLORD J SEBENS ·
HURLEY A SMITH ·
DEEN · JOHNNIE N SHEARES Jr ·
JAMES W DUK
WALLACE L GI
JERRY W GLEG
37 E
Jeffrey T. Cochran

In 2014, when Jeff crashed his bike and suffered a Traumatic Brain Injury (TBI), his memories of Vietnam were lightened, and he was able to remember more of his childhood. He began to tell me stories from when he was a kid that I had never heard before. It was fun to see this side of him, and to see the simple joy of remembering the fun he used to have before Vietnam. He also started eating meat again. He'd been a vegetarian for nearly 40 years, and after his TBI he asked me, "Now, why is it I don't eat meat?" His first bite was bacon. That was the end of his vegetarianism. And for the rest of his life, he thoroughly enjoyed eating meat!

Although it was a relief that the constant memories of Vietnam were gone, he had a new issue. He became fixated on the fact that he had killed people and that he could never be forgiven for what he had done. He couldn't forgive himself, nor did he think anyone could absolve him of this burden. No matter how much I tried to convince him that it was totally out of his control and that he had been drafted and trained to be a soldier on the front lines, and it was a kill or be killed situation, he would not accept it. In his mind, he had participated in the killing of human beings and no matter the circumstances, that would never be okay.

In the months before he passed, we talked about it often and he held such deep pain for those lives he ended. He understood he was a Marine and that was what he was trained to do, but with all the layers of protection stripped away by his TBI, all he had left was remorse and nearly unbearable guilt. It broke my heart, and I wanted so badly to ease his pain. In the last few days of his life, I whispered in his ear every time, just before I left his room, "You are Safe, You are Loved, and You are Forgiven." Sometimes he smirked at me, other times I held him as he cried.

When he told me that he had had enough and made the decision to stop eating, I knew. I knew he was ready to go and was through. His brain, from the stokes and the TBI, had betrayed him, and he was left feeling confused, angry, sad, and in deep emotional pain. The decision to go on Hospice was one he made by his actions and his decision to stop eating. As much as it hurt, I had to support him. He was ready to go. And he did.

Now he is free.

Jeff's Last Thoughts

During the process of preparing this book, I decided to get away and booked a hotel for three nights. My goal was to focus on Jeff's book and get it finished. It was a great idea, and I was able to get lots of work done.

On the second night, I awoke startled; I had this powerful feeling that Jeff was trying to tell me something. I know how odd this sounds, but it was very real. I wasn't sure what to do, so I grabbed a pad and pencil and just started writing what was coming to me. Here is what I wrote.

"The title of the book should be, The United States Marine Corps Gave Me a Mental Illness and Poisoned Me, Too.

What I want to tell my family and the people who know me is that going to war – experiencing war – was so traumatic that it gave me a mental illness. That mental illness was the center of my life.

PTSD is a mental illness. I was ashamed of that. Having a mental illness is looked on with questioning glances and raised eyebrows.

But this is not a shortcoming of me, or some weakness – it was caused by witnessing horrific events in life-threatening circumstances that were too much for my brain, which was really not fully formed, to handle. It caused my mind to become ill. This sickness was caused by the United States Marine Corps – an agent for the Military Industrial Complex that profits from war.

I was a pawn in the machine. Labeled and pitted – a "Crazy Vietnam Vet."

When I was in Vietnam, I interacted with the people living in the villages, and I was exposed to a new way of looking at life. They were Buddhist. This was something I never knew existed. Being exposed to such a different culture allowed me to see beyond the veil of war and see humanity. I could see beyond being an American Marine fighting against Communism and saw the real truth – the senselessness of the war and who it was really hurting.

When I came home, I could no longer support the country in the way I had when I left. Patriotism seemed like condoning the war, and that was impossible for me. That is why it took me so long to get help from the VA or apply for benefits. After returning, I could never say the Pledge of Allegiance or stand for the National Anthem. I know other vets felt overly patriotic, but I could not."

This was Jeff. It was what he said to me on innumerable occasions. As a matter of fact, he used to joke a lot about being a "crazy Vietnam vet." It was his way of dealing with it. He used to hate it when people thanked him for his service or called him a hero. He would always be polite, but afterwards he would grumble about it and remark that he shouldn't be thanked for killing people. Of course, he understood that they weren't thanking him for that – but in his mind what he had done and what he had seen was nothing to be thanked for.

He also realized that the people in his life, especially his family, felt a heightened sense of patriotism because of his sacrifice. Again, he understood that but could not feel that level of it for himself. He had experienced war in a way most people have not. I remember in the 90s seeing him scrap off the bumper stickers he has on his truck – anything to do with Vietnam or the Marine Corps. I asked him why he was doing that, and he told me, "I can't identify with that anymore, it is not who I am."

The Stress Letter

As part of the application process for compensation from the Veteran's Administration (VA), Jeff had to submit a list of events that he felt contributed to his PTSD. It took us several weeks to go through this process, as it was very difficult for him to talk about. This was the first time I had heard these stories in their full version. He spoke briefly over the years of some of the incidents, but this was different. He had to look at them in the context of how they affected him physiologically and psychologically.

As he talked, I typed. We stopped a lot and there was a lot of crying and holding each other. The sadness and pain this evoked was difficult (for us both). As I look back now, I am so grateful for this experience, because I believe it helped him so much. Just getting it out and sharing it.

These incidents were the events he wanted to attempt to heal in the Trauma Processing Group that never happened. So, this was a mini version. Afterwards, he was clear that he wanted to share this with his son, brother, and sisters. He felt it would help them better understand why he was so different when he returned from Vietnam and why he was so troubled.

NOTE: Be aware these are graphic descriptions.

Stress Events – Letter Sent to VA for Determination for Compensation

Date:12/15/67
Location: Near City of Hoa An – Firebase
Unit: 1st Battalion, 5th Marines, 1st Marine Division, FMF

The incident that occurred on 12/15/67 is the one I remember and relive the most. After coming off combat operations for several weeks we were moved to a new firebase, which was the first time we had lived above ground for five months. The area was supposed to be secure, but I felt very uneasy about being vulnerable sleeping above ground. Things were fine for a few days, then on that night an 81mm, high explosive mortar round hit the top framing of our tent causing an airburst to shower down shrapnel on two squads.

Everything went crazy, there were people screaming, one guy was killed instantly, blood was everywhere. We rolled as fast as we could into the bunkers at the edge of the tents. Once we realized there were no more rounds being fired, we rushed in to take care of the guys who couldn't move.

Medivac choppers arrived within ten minutes from DaNang and evacuated us to the Naval Hospital in DaNang. We landed on a black top landing zone and the stretchers were immediately moved to a triage area. That area consisted of sloped concrete slab with four poles and metal roofing, bare light bulbs hanging from the ceiling. The stretches were put on sawhorses and the doctors and orderlies were running around checking for the most seriously wounded. They assigned causalities to different operating rooms.

I was "walking wounded" so was put off to last. I watched them work on Robert Olsen until he died. And I saw them carry all the guys in my squad off in different directions, to operating rooms. They were all very seriously wounded.

While the Corpsman were looking at my wounds, I was watching them hose down the blood and body parts of my fellow Marines with a garden hose down the big drain in the sloping concrete slab. I thought it looked like a butcher shop, but only the meat was people.

I never saw any of those guys again. It wasn't until I requested my records a few year ago that I found the information about the incident—two killed and twenty-four wounded. This is one of the incidents that I relive. I can see it clearly in my mind, I see the colors, smell the jungle and feel the night heat.

I was hospitalized for a month. While convalescing, I was made to do clean-up work in the intensive care ward of the hospital, where the most seriously wounded were cared for. I remember seeing a guy with his face half shot off, a guy with no legs, a guy who lost an arm, head wounds, you name it, I saw it. These scenes come back to me frequently in my dreams.

One month from the date of this incident I was sent back to my unit – but there were a bunch of new men in it. The unit had moved from Hoa An to Phu Loc. This firebase was in a valley at the base of the Aush Shau Valley. The whole battalion was under mortar and rocket attack at least 3-4 times a week.

Date: Mid-January 1968
Location: Phu Loc Firebase
Unit: 1st Battalion, 5th Marines, 1st Marine Division, FMF

The battalion was responsible for bridge security on Hwy 1 from Hai Van Pass to Phu Bai and for minesweeping the road between all the little villes and bridges, every day. Two men from every company were assembled to perform this minesweeping activity every day. So, the day I was picked I checked out an M60 machine gun, got my gear, and got on the truck. Our truck was the lead truck in the sweep. There was a driver, one man riding shotgun, and an engineer on each running board. I was in the bed of the truck with my machine gun resting on the roof. There were 5 other guys in the back of the bed with rifles, grenade launchers, etc., armed to the hilt.

We left the gate of the firebase, driving very slowly, the engineers would get down and check anything in the road that looked suspicious. Less than a quarter of a mile after we left the main gate, an enemy solider set off a command detonated mine on our truck. There was a bright flash. The engineer next to me on the running board was cut in half and disappeared in the smoke and dirt. We jumped off the truck, firing wildly into the bushes thinking it was the start of an ambush. But the enemy solider ran away and there was no further action.

On returning to the truck, we found the guy riding shotgun was also killed, the driver and several others were badly wounded. I was less than two feet from both of the men that were killed instantly.

The guy who was acting as my assistant gunner pointed to the machine gun ammo I had draped across my shoulders and pointed to three bullets that had been cut open by shrapnel – the gun powder was leaking out – it was inches from my throat. After this numbing 81 mortar incident in December, these deaths seemed somehow easier. My emotions were shutting down.

This event is still relived in my dreams, yet today.

Date: Mid-January 1968
Location: Ville outside Phu Loc Firebase – Hwy 1 Bridge Security
Unit: 1st Battalion, 5th Marines, 1st Marine Division, FMF

We had just relieved the 2nd Battalion, 2nd Marines from the bridge security. We moved into the village late in the afternoon with only the equipment that was on our backs. We were unfamiliar with this area. That night we were attacked by a VC Sapper Squad, followed by a ground attack that swept through the ville and blew up the bridge.

My squad was in the schoolhouse about 100 feet from the bridge. The Sappers crawled through the barbed wire right up to the small wall where the bunkers were built for bridge defense. They threw satchel charges into all the main bunkers and blew them up. The VC had a B40 rocket team across the road in the tower of a church. They were shooting rockets down into the compound where we were in the trench line trying to defend our corner of the school. There were South Vietnamese soldiers fighting with us – they lived in this little village – this was their home. They were on the line, near the wall. The rocket team was taking out one small bunker after another with each rocket.

After they had suppressed our return fire, they swept through the ville throwing hand grenades and shooting until the bridge was blown up. We were just trying to stay alive. We were hanging on for dear life. Just before dawn they broke off the engagement and retreated back into the jungle. By this time, we got out of the trench to check for dead and wounded. The battle was over.

The two South Vietnamese in the bunker closest to our trench line were blown apart by a direct hit from a B40 rocket. They looked like broken mannequins. Their skin was so pale that they didn't look real. When we checked the barbed wire on the other side of the wall, there were five dead VC Sappers caught in the wire. Several Marines were buried in the blown-up bunkers. We had to dig them out by hand. Two of them were still alive. There were several killed and many wounded.

By the time of this incident, I was completely shut down and their deaths had hardly any meaning to me at all. However, I still can vividly see their faces today, as if it were yesterday.

Date: Mid-February 1968
Location: Hue City – Tet Offensive
Unit: 1st Battalion, 5th Marines, 1st Marine Division, FMF

About mid-February our battalion was ordered into Hue City. We got our gear, got on trucks and drove outside the city. We moved through the south side of the city, crossed the Perfume River, and headed for the Citadel, which looked like a giant wall.

For the next three weeks I was afraid of dying 24-hours a day. We had never been in a city before, like a real city – streets, houses, cars, gas stations, etc. Before, we had always just fought in the jungle. Within days the fighting seems to be everywhere. There were snipers in every direction, random shooting, artillery attacks, mortar fire, hand grenades, B40 rockets day after day, after day. We were losing people right and left, the line companies were cut to pieces. We would shoot our mortars at them, and they would shoot their mortars back at us.

Our gun team would set up in the courtyard of a house for a few hours or even two or three days and fire support for the line companies moving through streets, house by house. People were being killed or wounded constantly. The fighting was heavy in the daytime and would slack off at night. Everyone would consolidate their positions and get ready for the next day. After a week or so, we thought none of us would get out alive. But, by mid-March it was over.

When they pulled us out, we heard that 150 had been killed and 850 wounded. However, it seems like much more than that to me. (The actual totals were: 216 US Marines killed and 1609 wounded. Civilian deaths were staggering – 14,000 killed and 24,000 wounded. The deadliest week of the entire war for the USA was during the Tet Offensive, specifically February 11-17, 1968, during which period 543 Americans were killed in action, and 2547 were wounded.)

If I close my eyes, I can go back there and relive those weeks instantly. The feelings of extreme fear, loss, hopelessness and helplessness that I felt in Hue City in 1968 has never been far from me throughout my entire life.

Along with this Stress Letter, Jeff had to take a series of tests, be interviewed by several doctors, a psychologist, and a physiatrist. We both had to be interviewed by a panel of VA officials and then had to wait several months to learn the outcome. We started the process in 2000 and he was initially given 30% disability for Agent Orange Exposure and PTSD. We appealed and had to go through another long process and finally he was approved for 100% disability in 2004. This process took a huge toll on Jeff. Having to talk about and relive the experiences caused him a lot of anguish. He was glad he did it, and it certainly improved his (our) life, but it was a long and difficult process.

In the next section are the results of all the tests, interviews and doctor visits.

Psychological Report

Compensation and Pension (C&P) Exam

Findings as reported by VA Clinical Psychologist Dr. Bolger.

Mr. Cochran presents as an attractive, physically fit man who remained fairly anxious and fidgety through most of the evaluation. Affect was blunted, mood sad and depressed. He did not smile and acknowledged anhedonia (Inability to experience pleasure from activities usually found enjoyable) and depression. At several points in the interview, he appeared to be holding back tears, particularly in regard to his embarrassment with losing work contracts and failing to contribute to the family income. His insight into his disorder, including the pros and cons of psychotherapeutic treatment of PTSD, was very good, and he acknowledged that he might have to experience bad feelings for a while to be able to experience good feeling in the future. Yet, he seemed to have difficulty recognizing the difficulties he was having in his job and was unable to estimate his current or previous income. It became clear that he has given his wife complete responsibility for the running of the household and dealing with financial matters. His wife agreed that she has become responsible for "everything." At times, Mr

Cochran appeared to be having difficulty recalling recent specific events, justifying his failure to do so as an attempt to "minimize" the extent of his problems. Yet, there was no evidence of thought disorder or paranoia, and he expressed himself well, appearing of average to above average intellect.

Mr. Cochran is experiencing the following symptoms of PTSD:

Re-experiencing Cluster – Mr. Cochran re-experiences traumatic events of Vietnam on a daily basis. While the winter months have always been hard for him because his trauma occurred during that season of year, he finds that lately he thinks about "ambush sites" while looking out over the lush, green vegetation during summer. His wife verified that thoughts about Vietnam have dramatically increased. "Everything reminds him of Vietnam," she said. Actual re-enactment experiences have increased from approximately two times per month to weekly and are usually associated with hearing helicopters or sensing "that damp jungle smell." During these periods, he experiences panic attacks including hyperventilation, racing heartbeat, and excessive perspiration. He also fears seeing fog and avoids being out too early in the morning or late at night to reduce the change of the re-enactment at that time. Nightmares are nightly (confirmed by his wife). They are quite realistic and lead to crying out and perspiration. Significant to note, for the past year he no longer sleeps under the sheets with his wife but puts a sleeping bag on top of the covers or sleeps in the sleeping bag on the floor. He feels safer.

Avoidance Cluster – To help sleep, Mr. Cochran uses a noise machine to try to drown out sounds that immediately wake him up and interfere with his sleep. Still, he often gets a feeling that he needs to get up and check something going on outside. Most nights, he sleeps approximately three hours, tosses and turns until daybreak. He naps during the days. The couple lives in a basement apartment with small windows. He pulls the shades closed in the evenings, feeling safer because "there is ground on the other side of the walls." Veteran continues to carry a knife but indicates that he has been slowly reducing the size of the blade. Mrs. Cochran expressed that he still appears obsessed with knives however, and he spends hours filing a pouch of knives that he wears around. The couple feels that he has made some improvement in two areas, however. He feels less irritable than in the past, less capable of anger, and less susceptible to startle, although significantly more depressed. However, both are concerned about the severity of concentration difficulties that have significantly worsened in the last six months

For example, the veteran forgot to pay his phone bill on the company phone, the phone was disconnected for several months while he wondered why he wasn't getting any call for work. He lost another contract job when he attempted to change a florescent light at the daycare center

Apparently, the light was in a room of babies in their cribs, and without asking for the cribs to be removed, he attempted to change the light. It dropped to the floor, send shards of glass into the cribs. "I just lose the program," Mr. Cochran state, "even when I am trying to do something, I've done a lot in the past." His wife reports that things have gotten to the point that his hygiene is slipping, he will stay in the same clothes for days, and needs reminders to bathe.

Tests Administered/Results: In addition to the clinical interview, Mr. Cochran completed the MMPI-2. Results suggest that Mr. Cochran approached the test with honesty, without any evidence of an attempt to purposely exaggerate symptoms of psychopathology. The overall pattern suggests that Mr. Cochran is currently experiencing extreme stress and discomfort, and subscale elevations are typical of the pattern shown by veterans diagnosed with PTSD (7,8,2 triad). The PTSD subscale (PK) show a raw score of 38, ten points higher than the cut-off used to diagnosis of PTSD in

Vietnam veterans. Individuals with similar profiles are experiencing fairly severe levels of stress, anxiety, depression and alienation. They often feel anxious, agitated, tense, and jumpy. Sleep disturbance, inability to concentrate, confused thinking and forgetfulness is also characteristic. There is also a tendency to feel a loss of control over the environment. This pattern of responses is also seen in individuals with blunted affect who are withdrawn and socially self-isolating. These individuals often feel inadequate, inferior, and guilty when their stands for themselves are not met.

Findings: Mr. Cochran's reported history, presentation in this interview and objective testing support a diagnosis of PTSD. This veteran is found to suffer a mental disorder, leading to disabling occupational and social impairment. While his C-file was unavailable to verify the couple's statement for worsening functioning compared to only two years ago, he appears to be experiencing significant difficulties coping at the present time. He has lost most (if not all) of his contracts as a handy man and lives his life in the seclusion of a basement apartment. There is a report of declined hygiene and worsening intrusive thoughts about Vietnam. At present, he seems quite dependent on his wife and he has relied heavily upon her to handle his financial affairs. While the veteran does have several risk factors for vascular disease, the onset and course of cognitive dysfunction appears too raid for vascular disease, the onset and course of cognitive dysfunction appears too rapid for a typical presentation of Dementia. Yet, at the present time, I cannot totally rule out an organic component to his cognitive complaints and neurological (and possibly neuropsychological) evaluation is indicated.

John P. Bolger, Ph.D.
Clinical Psychologist

History and Combat Record

8/16/66 Date of entry into the USMC

8/16/66 -12/17/66 Boot Camp, Camp Lejeune, NC

1/6/67 – 5/6/67 Guantanamo Bay, Cuba

7/22/67 Arrived DaNang, Republic of Vietnam

Combat History July 1967 – July 1968

7/29/67 Participated in Operations against insurgence Communist Viet Cong Forces in the RVN (Republic of Viet Nam)

8/27/67 Participated in Operation Cochise, vicinity of Quang Nam Province, RVN

9/12/67 Participated in Operation Swift, vicinity of Quang Nam Province, RVN

11/13/67 Participated in Operation Onslow, vicinity of Quang Nam Province, RVN

12/14/67 Participated in Operation "Junction", vicinity of Quang Nam Province, RVN

12/67-1/68 Hospitalized

2/12/68 Participated in Operation Hue City (Tet Offensive), vicinity of Thua Thien Province

3/5/68 Participated in Operation Houston #1, vicinity of Thua Thien Province, RVN

4/21/68 Participated in Operation Baxter Garden, vicinity of Thua Thien Province, RVN

5/1-31/68 Participated in Operation Houston II, vicinity of Thua Thien Province, RVN

6/1-30/68 Participated in Operation Houston III, vicinity of Thua Thien Province, RVN

7/1-9/68 Participated in Operation Houston IV, vicinity of Thua Thien Province, RVN

7/9-19/68 Participated in Operation Mameluke Thrust, vicinity of Quang Nam Province, RVN

8/5/68 Left Da Nang, Republic of Vietnam

8/8/68 Arrived Travis Air Force Base, CA

9/4/68 Stationed at Camp Pendleton, USMC Base, CA

6/13/69 Honorably Discharged from active duty:21G-Convenience of the Government

Decorations

National Defense Service Metal

Vietnamese Service Medal 3*

Vietnamese Campaign Medal w/Device

Presidential Unit Citation

Combat Action Ribbon

Good Conduct Metal

Purple Heart (Never officially awarded)

Photos and Historical Memorabilia

AUG • 68

AUG • 68

AUG 68

AUG • 68

AUG • 68

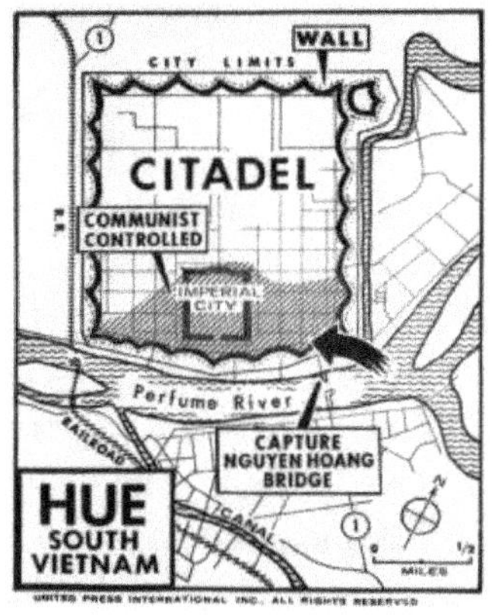

"Combat in a built-up area is close, personal and extremely violent."

— Maj. Bob Thompson, Commander 1st Battalion, 5th Marine Regiment

U.S. Marines, Hue City, January, 1968

Zia's Final Thoughts

I was born into a family where the effects of war have played a huge role in both family lines. My mother lost a brother in WWII. He was a tailgunner in the US Air Force and his plane was shot down in the South Pacific. Others on the plane were rescued, but because my uncle was in the tail of the plane it was impossible for them to save him. He drowned. His parents and my mother, his sister, were devastated and never fully mourned his loss. Ever.

My father was in the US Marine Corps during WWII and fought in some of the bloodiest battles in the South Pacific. He returned home with "shellshock". They didn't have a diagnosis for it then, but he was suffering from Post Traumatic Stress Disorder. He had many of the same symptoms that Jeff suffered. I was raised by that man. I understood what it was like to live with someone with PTSD, although I really didn't completely understand it as a kid. But by the time I got together with Jeff, I was well aware. That is how we connected. He knew that I got it, that I understand in a way most people don't. I was safe for him. And we had a connection that was deep. It wasn't an ordinary relationship.

My father's PTSD clouded his life, his relationships, his family bonds, and his self-image, just like Jeff. So, I understand the effects of war from different perspective than most people.

When I reflect on the 20 years of life with my father, and 34 years with Jeff, I believe I can say that I see how war and its effects devastate a lot of people beyond the veteran.

However, the veteran has to live with it 24/7. It never goes away, and they are identified as the "issue", which I know makes it even harder. They don't want to hurt the people they love or have to continually deal with memories, flashbacks, and seasonal or situational triggers. They don't want to struggle with issues of anger and rage, like my Dad, or dark bouts of depression and isolation, like Jeff and my Dad. They just signed up to serve their country and do their patriotic duty.

People often asked me why Jeff just couldn't let it go. I often thought that myself. I remember reading about Senator John McCain, who was a POW for 5 ½ years and suffered continual torture and abuse. But when he returned home, he seemed to get his life together and ran for public office. I thought to myself, "how could that guy be okay and Jeff still be so broken?" That isn't even a fair comparison, and I am ashamed of myself for thinking it, but I wondered.

I don't know John McCain, but I know Jeff. After many years of experience and lots of reflection I have come to understand it. First, I will go back to the story Jeff told me about his 12th birthday. His father gave him a pellet gun, and that same day he killed a Cardinal. He told me that he knew, because of that incident, he could never be a hunter. The deep feeling of pain he felt about killing an animal impacted him profoundly. Because Jeff was at his core a kind, loving, gentle person. Far too gentle to kill animals. He spent his childhood helping his family, taking care of his siblings, helping neighbors, and always offering to help someone in need. His heart was huge and his feelings were deep. He was a sensitive soul.

In the years before his bike cash and TBI he used to talk about what his life would be like if he hadn't gone to war. He also said that if he had to do it all over again, he would have gone to Canada to avoid the draft. He was ashamed to say that to anyone else, because he didn't want people to think of him in that way. But he said that because he had grown to understand himself; he knew the gentleness of his nature, and his adversity to violence. Those traits came before Vietnam. They were innate within him. He knew that and understood it.

That is why I believe Jeff suffered from such severe PTSD. What it took to change that kind, loving, gentle soul into a solider and send him into war to kill people was more than his psyche could handle. He could never recover from that. He can never forget what he had done. He could not "get over it."

It is this reason for this book. To share his story. To expose his truth for others to try and understand and see what war does to a person.

> **"We were not allowed to speak of the unseen wounds of war. We were not allowed to prepare for them."** -Army Psychologist Brig. General Loree Sutton

While he was in hospice, we talked one night. He said that maybe in his next life he could come back and live a normal life, one not clouded in memories of war. He would have a big family, several kids, and maybe be a psychologist. He said he'd specialize in helping people recover from trauma.

"Wouldn't that be cool?" he said, with a smile.

I agreed.

During the last few days in Hospice Jeff and I talked about life after death. He seemed at peace about making the transition. I asked him to think of way he could let me know he was okay once he made it to the other side. A few days later, out of the blue, he said, "I figured out how to communicate with you. Anytime you see a squirrel acting crazy you'll know that's me." I laughed and told him I would be on the look out. Oddly enough, the day I was in Washington, DC at The Wall, this little guy (pictured above) was jumping around by the entrance and followed me along the walkway. It was weird, but I looked at him, and with a tear in my eye I said, "Come on Jeff, let's do this! You're finally here."

www.ingramcontent.com/pod-product-compliance
Lightning Source LLC
LaVergne TN
LVHW011048110826
845149LV00015B/3402

* 9 7 8 0 9 9 9 2 1 3 3 4 6 *